chinese **astrology**

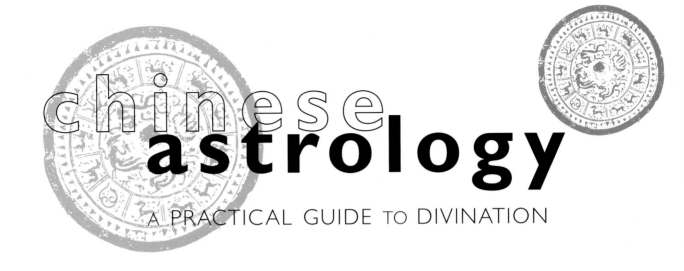

chinese astrology

A PRACTICAL GUIDE TO DIVINATION

richard craze

southwater

This edition is published by Southwater

Southwater is an imprint of
Anness Publishing Limited
Hermes House
88-89 Blackfriars Road
London
SE1 8HA
tel. 020 7401 2077
fax 020 7633 9499

Distributed in the USA by
Anness Publishing Inc.
27 West 20th Street
Suite 504
New York
NY10011
tel. 212 807 6739
fax 212 807 6813

Distributed in the UK by
The Manning Partnership
251-253 London Road East
Batheaston
Bath
BA1 7RL
tel. 01225 852 727
fax 01225 852 852

Distributed in Australia by
Sandstone Publishing
Unit 1
360 Norton Street
Leichhardt
New South Wales 2040
tel. 02 9560 7888
fax 02 9560 7488

3 5 7 9 10 8 6 4 2

Publisher: Joanna Lorenz
Project Editor: Joanne Rippin
Designer: Lesley Betts
Illustrator: Attic Publishing

Previously published as *The Chinese Astrology Handbook*

Contents

Introduction

According to legend, when the Buddha found enlightenment under a fig tree he invited all the animals to share in his joy. Only 12 accepted, however, and it is these who are honoured by being included in the Chinese zodiac. Each animal was allotted its own year to govern.

Chinese astrology is very old. Although the Buddha lived two and a half millennia ago (563–483BC), the truth is that no one actually knows how old it is. There are some who date the origin of Chinese astrology as far back as the Yellow Emperor, who reigned around 2630 BC. What we do know is that the system still in wide use today in China and other Eastern countries has remained unchanged for several thousands of years. Even until quite recently it would have been unthinkable to have got married, bought a house, changed jobs, conceived a child or even celebrated without some advice from an astrologer. And it wasn't so long before that when the Emperor of China banned "ordinary" people from using astrology at all on the grounds that it was dangerous. He considered the information it imparted to be so accurate that it could be used to plot against him and his court. So he simply banned its use – except for himself naturally.

A TIBETAN PAINTING SHOWING THE BUDDHA CUTTING HIS HAIR TO RENOUNCE THE WORLD.

LEFT: AN EIGHTEENTH-CENTURY TIBETAN PAINTING OF THE LIFE OF BUDDHA, SHOWING HIS BIRTH, SEVEN STEPS AND BATH.

The Signs

I n China, if you wanted to get married, an astrologer would have drawn up a personal horoscope using such information as when you were born – the exact moment – not just the year, when your parents were born and any other relevant information he would need, such as the birth time and date of your fiancé.

The animal signs don't just govern the years. They are also allotted a month and a time of day when you were born. So, for instance, you wouldn't just be, say, a tiger – as that would only refer to your year. You might be a tiger according to the year, but a monkey according to the month of your birth, and a goat according to your time of birth. Each of these animals would bring their own characteristics to your chart. The characteristics of the 12 animals are briefly described here.

THE SIGNS
Rat – intelligent and practical
Ox – reliable and purposeful
Tiger – daring and passionate
Hare – intuitive and sensitive
Dragon – successful and independent
Snake – mysterious and sophisticated
Horse – hardworking and friendly
Goat – sexy and adaptable
Monkey – quick-witted and entertaining
Rooster – protective and honest
Dog – loyal and trustworthy
Pig – sensual and eager

ANIMAL QUALITIES

These animal qualities apply no matter whether it is the year, month or time of day we are looking at. Their combination makes you unique – you are no longer just a snake or a rooster but maybe a snake (year) monkey (month) rat (time of day). Or a rooster (year) tiger (month) horse (time of day).

Your year animal is the outer you – the part you show the outside world. Your month animal (known as your lunar animal) is you in relationships and love – your inner animal of the heart. And your time of day animal is the real you – the dark secret animal that you don't show the rest of the world.

RIGHT: A CHINESE CALENDAR, SURROUNDED BY ILLUSTRATIONS FROM THE HOROSCOPE.

The Philosophy of Chinese Astrology

Originally, Chinese astrology was influenced by Taoism which is the ancient religion of China. The Tao (the Way) says that everything in the universe has a quality or aspect which is either male or female, advancing or retiring, light or dark.

YIN AND YANG

These two opposites are called yang (male) and yin (female). Yang and yin each have many qualities: yang – hot, dry, active, day, positive, right, south, summer, fire, full; yin – cool, wet, passive, night, negative, left, north, winter, water, empty. These two opposites were illustrated by the yin/yang symbol. Each half of this symbol has a tiny dot of the opposite aspect within itself to show that each grows into its opposite. That is the fundamental philosophy of the Tao – everything is in a state of constant change – from yin to yang; from yang to yin. These two qualities are not in conflict with each other but rather are complementary; we cannot do without either of them and together they make us complete.

FAR LEFT: THE YIN YANG SYMBOL.

LEFT: A SEVENTEENTH-CENTURY CHINESE PAINTING SHOWING A GROUP OF MIXED AGES STUDYING THE YIN YANG SYMBOL.

The Five Elements

WATER
THE NORTH
COMMUNICATION,
SENSITIVITY
AND INTUITION

WOOD
THE EAST
NURTURING,
CREATIVITY AND
GROWTH

The basic quality of yin or yang can then be further defined by being one of the five elements – water, wood, fire, metal or earth. Each of these elements has a quality which applies to both animals and years. Each of the 12 animals of the Chinese zodiac is governed by an element and a yin or yang direction. They are divided into four groups of three: water – rat, ox, pig; wood – tiger, hare and dragon; fire – snake, horse and goat; metal – monkey, rooster and dog. Earth, being the centre, doesn't rule any animals but it does lend its qualities to some of the years. So each year has its animal, its yin or yang aspect and its element.

METAL
THE WEST
USEFUL, STRONG
AND DEPENDABLE

EARTH
THE CENTRE
BALANCE,
RELIABILITY,
FOUNDATIONS

FIRE
THE SOUTH
PASSION,
INTELLIGENCE AND
MOVEMENT

The Sixty Year Cycle

As there are 12 animals and five elements in the Chinese astrological system, this gives us a 60-year cycle, with half of the years being yin and half being yang. This 60-year cycle is important as it makes each year of the 60 special and unique – you aren't just a particular animal (one of 12) but a particular type of animal, perhaps a yang water tiger which is very different from a yang wood tiger. If we then add in the 12 months and the 12 times of day divisions we can see that there are a total of 8640 combinations of horoscopes (five elements x 12 animals x 12 months x 12 times of day).

How to Use Chinese Astrology

Each of the 12 animals rules a particular year in rotation. In addition to lending its characteristics to people born during that year it also influences the quality of the year – which affects us all. As we all have to endure or enjoy each of the years, knowing which animal rules a future year can help us to plan in advance for the trials and triumphs that year might bring. For instance, the year of the dragon is usually associated with expansion and prosperity, and so we might be advised to speculate or start new businesses in a dragon year, whereas during a hare year, which is associated with introspection and learning, we might be advised to start a new course of study and leave business expansion plans to a later dragon year.

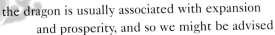

LEFT: AN EIGHTEENTH-CENTURY PAINTING OF A CHINESE MANDARIN.

ANIMAL MONTHS AND HOURS
Rat – December – 11pm – 1am

Ox – January – 1am – 3am

Tiger – February – 3am – 5am

Hare – March – 5am – 7am

Dragon – April – 7am – 9am

Snake – May – 9am – 11am

Horse – June – 11am – 1pm

Goat – July – 1pm – 3pm

Monkey – August – 3pm – 5pm

Rooster – September – 5pm – 7pm

Dog – October – 7pm – 9pm

Pig – November – 9pm – 11pm

YOUR INNER AND SECRET ANIMALS
You have more than one animal sign, however, and it is important that you work out your inner and secret animals too. Your inner animal is worked out by the month in which you were born – the lunar month. This controls your love life, so if you want to find out whether you are compatible with another sign, you need to know both your own inner animal and your potential partner's. Your secret animal is determined by the time of your birth, and it is this animal which will reveal the true you – to yourself only of course. So if you were born at 08.00, February 1963, outwardly you are a hare, your inner animal is the tiger, and your secret animal is the dragon.

Astrological Compatibility

This information enables us to know what each year could bring us (and each month) and it is easy also to check what sort of people are around us. Suppose we are considering going into business with a friend, for instance. We know what animal he or she is and what sort of animal we are – so are the two compatible? Would a pig make a good business partner for a rat? Look at the compatibility chart below for a quick at-a-glance check, and use the same information for relationships; are you compatible with your lover? You can even use the charts to look at friendships, the compatibilities don't change.

A CHINESE FAMILY ON THE VERANDA OF THEIR HOME IN 1845.

Each of the animals is said to have two close friends and one deadly enemy. The two close friends are identified by counting round four animals in each direction from your sign, the deadly enemy is the animal directly opposite you. The other two signs that make up that particular element aren't too good to associate with either. Once we know what each animal represents we can use that information to plan better, more rewarding and fulfilling lives for ourselves and our families.

Year Charts

Each of the animals has five different and distinct personalities depending on which element it is – and that depends on the year you were born. Look up your relevant year and read the introduction to that animal – and then read about the individual element of the animal.

The Years and Their Signs

Year	From - to	Aspect	Element	Animal sign
1900	31 Jan 1900 - 18 Feb 1901	Yang	Metal	Rat
1901	19 Feb 1901 - 7 Feb 1902	Yin	Metal	Ox
1902	8 Feb 1902 - 28 Jan 1903	Yang	Water	Tiger
1903	29 Jan 1903 - 15 Feb 1904	Yin	Water	Hare
1904	16 Feb 1904 - 3 Feb 1905	Yang	Wood	Dragon
1905	4 Feb 1905 - 24 Jan 1906	Yin	Wood	Snake
1906	25 Jan 1906 - 2 Feb 1907	Yang	Fire	Horse
1907	3 Feb 1907 - 1 Feb 1908	Yin	Fire	Goat
1908	2 Feb 1908 - 21 Jan 1909	Yang	Earth	Monkey
1909	22 Jan 1909 - 9 Feb 1910	Yin	Earth	Rooster
1910	10 Feb 1910 - 29 Jan 1911	Yang	Metal	Dog
1911	30 Jan 1911 - 17 Feb 1912	Yin	Metal	Pig
1912	18 Feb 1912 - 5 Feb 1913	Yang	Water	Rat
1913	6 Feb 1913 - 25 Jan 1914	Yin	Water	Ox
1914	26 Jan 1914 - 13 Feb 1915	Yang	Wood	Tiger

Year	From - to	Aspect	Element	Animal sign
1915	14 Feb 1915 - 2 Feb 1916	Yin	Wood	Hare
1916	3 Feb 1916 - 22 Jan 1917	Yang	Fire	Dragon
1917	23 Jan 1917 - 10 Feb 1918	Yin	Fire	Snake
1918	11 Feb 1918 - 31 Jan 1919	Yang	Earth	Horse
1919	1 Feb 1919 - 19 Feb 1920	Yin	Earth	Goat
1920	20 Feb 1920 - 7 Feb 1921	Yang	Metal	Monkey
1921	8 Feb 1921 - 27 Jan 1922	Yin	Metal	Rooster
1922	28 Jan 1922 - 15 Feb 1923	Yang	Water	Dog
1923	16 Feb 1923 - 4 Feb 1924	Yin	Water	Pig
1924	5 Feb 1924 - 24 Jan 1925	Yang	Wood	Rat
1925	25 Jan 1925 - 12 Feb 1926	Yin	Wood	Ox
1926	13 Feb 1926 - 1 Feb 1927	Yang	Fire	Tiger
1927	2 Feb 1927 - 22 Jan 1928	Yin	Fire	Hare
1928	23 Jan 1928 - 9 Feb 1929	Yang	Earth	Dragon
1929	10 Feb 1929 - 9 Jan 1930	Yin	Earth	Snake
1930	10 Jan 1930 - 16 Feb 1931	Yang	Metal	Horse
1931	17 Feb 1931 - 5 Feb 1932	Yin	Metal	Goat
1932	6 Feb 1932 - 25 Jan 1933	Yang	Water	Monkey
1933	26 Jan 1933 - 13 Feb 1934	Yin	Water	Rooster
1934	14 Feb 1934 - 3 Feb 1935	Yang	Wood	Dog
1935	4 Feb 1935 - 23 Jan 1936	Yin	Wood	Pig
1936	24 Jan 1936 - 10 Feb 1937	Yang	Fire	Rat
1937	11 Feb 1937 - 30 Jan 1938	Yin	Fire	Ox
1938	31 Jan 1938 - 18 Feb 1939	Yang	Earth	Tiger
1939	19 Feb 1939 - 7 Feb 1940	Yin	Earth	Hare
1940	8 Feb 1940 - 26 Jan 1941	Yang	Metal	Dragon
1941	27 Jan 1941 - 14 Feb 1942	Yin	Metal	Snake
1942	15 Feb 1942 - 4 Feb 1943	Yang	Water	Horse
1943	5 Feb 1943 - 24 Jan 1944	Yin	Water	Goat
1944	25 Jan 1944 - 12 Feb 1945	Yang	Wood	Monkey
1945	13 Feb 1945 - 1 Feb 1946	Yin	Wood	Rooster

Year	From - to	Aspect	Element	Animal sign
1946	2 Feb 1946 - 21 Jan 1947	Yang	Fire	Dog
1947	22 Jan 1947 - 9 Feb 1948	Yin	Fire	Pig
1948	10 Feb 1948 - 28 Jan 1949	Yang	Earth	Rat
1949	29 Jan 1949 - 16 Feb 1950	Yin	Earth	Ox
1950	17 Feb 1950 - 5 Feb 1951	Yang	Metal	Tiger
1951	6 Feb 1951 - 26 Jan 1952	Yin	Metal	Hare
1952	27 Jan 1952 - 13 Feb 1953	Yang	Water	Dragon
1953	14 Feb 1953 - 2 Feb 1954	Yin	Water	Snake
1954	3 Feb 1954 - 23 Jan 1955	Yang	Wood	Horse
1955	24 Jan 1955 - 11 Feb 1956	Yin	Wood	Goat
1956	12 Feb 1956 - 30 Jan 1957	Yang	Fire	Monkey
1957	31 Jan 1957 - 17 Feb 1958	Yin	Fire	Rooster
1958	18 Feb 1958 - 7 Feb 1959	Yang	Earth	Dog
1959	8 Feb 1959 - 27 Jan 1960	Yin	Earth	Pig
1960	28 Jan 1960 - 14 Feb 1961	Yang	Metal	Rat
1961	15 Feb 1961 - 4 Feb 1962	Yin	Metal	Ox
1962	5 Feb 1962 - 24 Jan 1963	Yang	Water	Tiger
1963	25 Jan 1963 - 12 Feb 1964	Yin	Water	Hare
1964	13 Feb 1964 - 1 Feb 1965	Yang	Wood	Dragon
1965	2 Feb 1965 - 20 Jan 1966	Yin	Wood	Snake
1966	21 Jan 1966 - 8 Feb 1967	Yang	Fire	Horse
1967	9 Feb 1967 - 29 Jan 1968	Yin	Fire	Goat
1968	30 Jan 1968 - 16 Feb 1969	Yang	Earth	Monkey
1969	17 Feb 1969 - 5 Feb 1970	Yin	Earth	Rooster
1970	6 Feb 1970 - 26 Jan 1971	Yang	Metal	Dog
1971	27 Jan 1971 - 15 Jan 1972	Yin	Metal	Pig
1972	16 Jan 1972 - 2 Feb 1973	Yang	Water	Rat
1973	3 Feb 1973 - 22 Jan 1974	Yin	Water	Ox
1974	23 Jan 1974 - 10 Feb 1975	Yang	Wood	Tiger
1975	11 Feb 1975 - 30 Jan 1976	Yin	Wood	Hare
1976	31 Jan 1976 - 17 Feb 1977	Yang	Fire	Dragon

Year	From - to	Aspect	Element	Animal sign
1977	18 Feb 1977 - 6 Feb 1978	Yin	Fire	Snake
1978	7 Feb 1978 - 27 Jan 1979	Yang	Earth	Horse
1979	28 Jan 1979 - 15 Feb 1980	Yin	Earth	Goat
1980	16 Feb 1980 - 4 Feb 1981	Yang	Metal	Monkey
1981	5 Feb 1981 - 24 Jan 1982	Yin	Metal	Rooster
1982	25 Jan 1982 - 12 Feb 1983	Yang	Water	Dog
1983	13 Feb 1983 - 1 Feb 1984	Yin	Water	Pig
1984	2 Feb 1984 - 19 Feb 1985	Yang	Wood	Rat
1985	20 Feb 1985 - 8 Feb 1986	Yin	Wood	Ox
1986	9 Feb 1986 - 29 Jan 1987	Yang	Fire	Tiger
1987	30 Jan 1987 - 16 Feb 1988	Yin	Fire	Hare
1988	17 Feb 1988 - 5 Feb 1989	Yang	Earth	Dragon
1989	6 Feb 1989 - 26 Jan 1990	Yin	Earth	Snake
1990	27 Jan 1990 - 14 Feb 1991	Yang	Metal	Horse
1991	15 Feb 1991 - 3 Feb 1992	Yin	Metal	Goat
1992	4 Feb 1992 - 22 Jan 1993	Yang	Water	Monkey
1993	23 Jan 1993 - 9 Feb 1994	Yin	Water	Rooster
1994	10 Feb 1994 - 30 Jan 1995	Yang	Wood	Dog
1995	31 Jan 1995 - 18 Feb 1996	Yin	Wood	Pig
1996	19 Feb 1996 - 7 Feb 1997	Yang	Fire	Rat
1997	8 Feb 1997 - 27 Jan 1998	Yin	Fire	Ox
1998	28 Jan 1998 - 15 Feb 1999	Yang	Earth	Tiger
1999	16 Feb 1999 - 4 Feb 2000	Yin	Earth	Hare
2000	5 Feb 2000 - 23 Jan 2001	Yang	Metal	Dragon
2001	24 Jan 2001 - 11 Feb 2002	Yin	Metal	Snake
2002	12 Feb 2002 - 31 Jan 2003	Yang	Water	Horse
2003	1 Feb 2003 - 21 Jan 2004	Yin	Water	Goat
2004	22 Jan 2004 - 8 Feb 2005	Yang	Wood	Monkey
2005	9 Feb 2005 - 28 Jan 2006	Yin	Wood	Rooster
2006	29 Jan 2006 - 17 Feb 2007	Yang	Fire	Dog
2007	18 Feb 2007 - 6 Feb 2008	Yin	Fire	Pig

The Rat

Rats are cheerful and industrious. They bounce back from setbacks quickly and easily and even when they are down they manage to keep smiling. Because of their reputation for being self-motivated they are often mistrusted, but they provide very well for their family, love their partners loyally and make good parents. They love to haggle for bargains and genuinely adore collecting money – and why not? Rats do always have a hidden agenda though, which can lead to them not being trusted – sometimes quite rightly so, for the rat fends primarily for itself.

ELEMENT:

WATER

YEARS OF THE RAT

1900 • 1912
1924 • 1936
1948 • 1960
1972 • 1984
1996 • 2008

CHARACTERISTICS

INTELLIGENT
•
PRACTICAL
•
PASSIONATE
•
SELF-INTERESTED
•
SENTIMENTAL

SUITABLE CAREERS

AUCTIONEER
•
MONEY LENDER
•
LAWYER
•
ANTIQUE DEALER
•
CAR SALESPERSON
•
FINANCIAL ADVISER

Rat Characteristics

Rats do not have a wider social conscience. They look after their own first. The rat is passionate and sentimental and regards a close, big family, well provided for, as their paradise. Rats like company and can be very practical. They're not given to much introspection. They can be very generous to their loved ones and have good taste.

THE RAT CAN BE VERY
PASSIONATE, AND ENJOYS THE
GAME OF SEDUCTION.

LOVE, SEX AND RELATIONSHIPS
Rats are sentimental, sensual and warm lovers. They will go out of their way to please their lovers and like to take the initiative when it comes to seduction. They are naturally faithful but need to be kept interested. As rats are naturally curious, spicing up your love-making with dark secret places, candlelight, good wines and plenty of surprises will ensure a rat stays with you forever. Allow it to be boring and the rat will vanish.

BUSINESS, FRIENDS AND CHILDREN
Rats are the hardworking entrepreneurs of the animal kingdom, and are clearly focused on money and success. They are outwardly charming and quick, and can fool people into thinking that they have the best interests of others at heart, but that is far from the truth. Rats are only interested in themselves and what they can acquire, steal, buy, obtain and accumulate. They hate to fail at anything and will always strive for success, measuring that success by how much they have acquired in material terms. This doesn't make rats bad people – merely greedy. They can turn any situation to their own advantage. Rats are usually popular and genuinely well liked, and usually have many friends. They adore their own children.

THE RAT LIKES TO BE
PART OF A BIG FAMILY AND
ENJOYS PROVIDING FOR
ITS MEMBERS.

THE RAT LIKES SECRET MEETINGS
AND INTRIGUE, AND WILL INDULGE
IN ILLICIT AFFAIRS AND
DANGEROUS LIAISONS WHENEVER
POSSIBLE.

The Five Rat Types

WATER RAT
This intuitive, adventurous rat likes to travel, but once it finds a safe haven, it will settle and won't be shifted. The water rat is creative, enjoys literature, and is a good diplomat.

WOOD RAT
Although hard-working and successful this is the least dynamic of the five rats and can be indecisive and prone to worry.

ALL RATS LIKE TO TRAVEL, BUT THEY ALSO ENJOY HOME-COMINGS AND DON'T LIKE TO BE AWAY FROM THEIR FAMILIES FOR TOO LONG.

FIRE RAT
This quick-witted, passionate rat has a flair for business, and the energy and enthusiasm to match. Unless it learns to curb its recklessness, it can be a bit dangerous.

THE WATER RAT IS THE ADVENTUROUS, MUCH TRAVELLED RAT

EARTH RAT
This serious, prudent rat likes practical problems with practical solutions. Although a bit of a plodder, it is usually successful, and makes a good accountant or financial advisor.

METAL RAT
Strong with fixed ideas, this rat can be stubborn, although it is helpful and hardworking. An ambitious rat, with the ability to see things through, it will be successful in all it undertakes.

THE METAL RAT IS INDUSTRIOUS AND HARDWORKING – AND THEREFORE TENDS TO BE VERY SUCCESSFUL.

Rat Compatibility Chart

RAT WITH:

RAT — A good combination as rats need a lot of attention – and are capable of giving lots in return. These two do well together in business or a relationship.

OX — A well balanced and harmonious partnership. The ox is a good listener and the rat will entertain him or her extremely well.

TIGER — As neither of these two knows how to compromise, this combination will create sparks and the relationship will be stormy.

HARE — The rat is a control freak while the hare dislikes control of any sort. Not a good combination.

DRAGON — A good relationship despite the apparent differences. Each will support the other in their schemes and will be able to give the other the attention they crave.

SNAKE — The snake's love of secrets and mysteries will inflame the rat to fits of jealousy and distrust. Not a good combination.

HORSE — Neither partner will get a word in edgeways – but if either can learn to listen the relationship does have potential.

GOAT — If the rat is allowed to control and be in charge then this could be a successful union. However, if the goat wants any freedom, the relationship is doomed.

MONKEY — These two characters are similar in personality and do well together. They are both starters rather than finishers and so will need to make allowances for that to do well together.

ROOSTER — With two control freaks, this combination just can't work. Neither partner will be interested in the other and both will demand to be in charge.

DOG — A good team. The rat's control and the dog's loyalty make a good combination, although they both like to talk a lot so the relationship could be a noisy one.

PIG — If the rat can earn it, the pig can spend it. As long as both know where they stand, this is a good partnership.

The Ox

The gentle giant of the animal world, the ox is a patient, kind person who takes responsibilities seriously, and expects everyone else to do so as well. The fact that often they don't puzzles the ox, who derives a lot of pleasure from doing things the right way – actually their own way. Oxen can be a bit set in their routines. They like to get up early and get on with their work, and they are tidy and well-organized. If you have a job that needs completing – no matter what it is – then assign it to an ox, and you won't be let down.

YEARS OF THE Ox

1901 • 1913
1925 • 1937
1949 • 1961
1973 • 1985
1997 • 2009

ELEMENT:

WATER

CHARACTERISTICS

RELIABLE
•
PURPOSEFUL
•
PATIENT
•
CONSCIENTIOUS

SUITABLE CAREERS

GARDENER
•
JUDGE
•
TEACHER
•
ESTATE MANAGER
•
CHEF
•
POLICE OFFICER

Ox Characteristics

The ox is a determined character with boundless energy and the capacity for some serious hard work. Totally reliable, an ox friend will always be there for you. Also patient, consistent and conscientious, an ox can sometimes be a bit dull and will occasionally need livening up. Basically a happy animal with few worries, the ox occasionally suffers from irrational fears, and needs lots of exercise and fresh air to prevent introspection. Oxen like to be appreciated and have their advice taken seriously. Don't ever laugh at an ox, or tease one – they just will not understand. This is a sensible, sober, traditional beast with an understanding of good old-fashioned virtues and hardly a vice at all.

LOVE, SEX AND RELATIONSHIPS

Being wary of emotion and too much excitement the ox is careful to avoid falling in love. But once an ox does fall in love, it's for life. Just don't expect too much romance – the ox is too down-to-earth for that, and being straightforward about sex, regards it as a practical necessity.

BUSINESS, FRIENDS AND CHILDREN

In business the ox can be ruthless and efficient, preferring to get on with the job in hand and hating wasting time, energy or money. Ox personalities make good parents as they have infinite patience and kindness. They also have many true friends who know they can depend on the ox in times of trouble. The ox is a very stable animal, and children, business partners and friends can all rely on the ox with total confidence.

THE OX IS A SERIOUS AND FAITHFUL LOVER AND PARTNER.

THE OX'S PATIENCE AND KINDLY PERSONALITY MAKES IT A VERY GOOD PARENT.

THE OX APPLIES ITSELF TO ITS WORK AND IS METHODICAL AND HARDWORKING.

The Five Ox Types

WATER OX

The diplomat ox knows how to listen and makes a good counsellor. Advice is freely given when asked for, and is usually good advice – especially about matters relating to love which will have been studied in great detail even if never personally experienced.

THE WATER OX KNOWS HOW TO LISTEN, AND MAKES A GOOD COUNSELLOR AND ADVISER.

WOOD OX

Blessed with a sense of humour, this laughing ox can be very witty. It is much more adaptable than the other ox types, with a need to try new things. The wood ox is volatile though and you should watch its temper.

FIRE OX

Unpredictable and dangerous, this is the bull in the china shop. When it has its head down and is working the fire ox is fine, but once it becomes bored or restless it can be extremely volatile – and its strength makes it worth watching out for.

THE OX DOES NOT MIX WELL WITH THE RASH AND IMPULSIVE HORSE.

EARTH OX

Earth oxen are resourceful and reliable. They make good researchers and scientists. They don't like to take risks and are careful and methodical. They accumulate great wealth through their hard work and endeavours.

ALL OXEN KNOW HOW TO WORK HARD, BUT THE EARTH OX IS THE HARDEST WORKER OF THEM ALL.

METAL OX

With considerable talents for organization, this very serious ox makes a good stage or office manager or a writer of business books. When a metal ox gives advice you'd better listen for it knows what it is talking about, especially when it comes to business.

Ox Compatibility Chart

Ox with:

RAT

Well balanced and harmonious. The ox is a good listener and the rat will entertain them both extremely well.

OX

Neither one of these two will have anything to say, and they will suffer each other in silence. This is not a good partnership.

TIGER

Unless the tiger allows the ox to be in control and set the rules this combination can't work. As tigers don't give in easily, expect fireworks.

HARE

The hare has a natural optimism that won't suit the ox who is pessimistic by nature. These two are badly suited.

DRAGON

A powerful combination. The ox can curb the dragon's impetuosity, and if they work as a team they can achieve anything together.

SNAKE

A good long-lasting and stable relationship. The snake understands the ox and will encourage them to lighten up – the ox gives the snake stability.

HORSE

This is not a good combination. The ox is thorough and methodical, while the horse is impulsive and rash. These two will irritate each other continually.

GOAT

These two won't agree on anything, and the ox will be appalled by the goat's apparent lack of morals.

MONKEY

The monkey constantly seeks change and the ox hates it. This combination can't work under any circumstances.

ROOSTER

The rooster sets things in motion and the ox will see them through. A good combination.

DOG

If both partners share the same goals, this can be a good partnership, but in business rather than love.

PIG

The ox will never tolerate the pig's spending habits, and the pig will consider the ox dull. Not a promising union.

The Tiger

YEARS OF THE
TIGER

1902 • 1914
1926 • 1938
1950 • 1962
1974 • 1986
1998 • 2010

Rash, impulsive and dynamic, tigers don't know how to sit still or calculate odds. They are bold, reckless and extremely foolish, and take risks that leave most of us gasping. But if you need a hero then a tiger will do fine. They like to take on the cause of the underdog and will fight against any injustice imaginable. Tigers are invariably charming and persuasive. The reason they are born leaders is not that they have any natural leading abilities, it's just that they can talk anyone into following them – no matter how ill-advised the project may be.

ELEMENT:
WOOD

CHARACTERISTICS

DARING
•
PASSIONATE
•
HEROIC
•
TENACIOUS
•
RECKLESS
•
FOOLISH

SUITABLE CAREERS

FILM STAR
•
ARMY OFFICER
•
WRITER
•
ATHLETE
•
POLITICIAN
•
RESTAURATEUR

Tiger Characteristics

The tiger is one of the most tenacious characters in the Chinese zodiac and very little will daunt tigers – or keep them down for long – they will always bounce back. They are not invulnerable, however, and need lots of emotional support, as they are basically insecure and can feel unloved.

TIGERS FALL IN LOVE
EASILY BUT MAKE
UNFAITHFUL AND
IMMORAL PARTNERS.

LOVE, SEX AND RELATIONSHIPS

Tigers have infinite resources of energy and imagination and will inevitably tire any lover they tangle with. They are promiscuous, adulterous and have absolutely no moral sense whatsoever and have no compunction about finding new excitement once the current relationship has begun to fade. They are great romantics, though, and fall in love easily and often. They do have a great capacity for very deep, intense relationships and are simply devastated when these fall apart, even if they are the cause. A tiger in love can be a rogue or simply perfect – and you'll never know which sort you're getting until it's too late.

THE TIGER LOVES TO BE
IN LOVE. TIGERS ARE
THE WORLD'S GREATEST
FLIRTS AND SEDUCERS.

BUSINESS, FRIENDS AND CHILDREN

Tigers are loners with few really good friends, but those they do have they keep for life. They make good parents; not because they set good examples, but because children just adore these exciting and charismatic personalities. They can be very strict and demanding, and do tend to expect a lot of their offspring.
In business, tigers are adventurous speculators, full of new ideas. They are good at starting new projects with enthusiasm and energy, but they do hate routine and get bored easily.

CHILDREN ADORE
TIGERS – AND TIGERS
ARE VERY FOND OF
CHILDREN TOO.

THE METAL TIGER
PROTECTS ITSELF WELL —
IT CAN BE RUTHLESS AND
SHOULDN'T BE CROSSED,
BUT IS A PUSSY CAT
AT HEART.

The Five Tiger Types

WATER TIGER

Possessing a greater sense of moral responsibility
than the others, this noble beast will often set a
good example and be fair and just. It can be a bit
pompous, though, and is very self-assured.
This is the calmest tiger.

WOOD TIGER

This social big cat is the life and soul of the party,
full of bright, entertaining ideas, but it's all a front –
this tiger is deeply insecure and feels unloved a
lot of the time. The wood tiger is the one most
likely to suffer from manic depression.

FIRE TIGER

The quickest and most ferocious of the tigers, the
fire tiger races everywhere as if it were on fire,
which internally it may well be. It needs to learn to
slow down and relax or it will burn out early.

EARTH TIGER

A tiger of extremely good taste, this
self-indulgent character recognizes quality and
likes to enjoy all the fine things in life. It can
run to fat if not careful, as it does enjoy good
food and fine wines. An earth tiger would
be an excellent food critic.

THE EARTH TIGER IS
THE REFINED TIGER OF
GOOD TASTE — IT CAN ALSO
BE RATHER SELF-
INDULGENT THOUGH.

THE WOOD TIGER IS THE
ULTIMATE PARTY
ANIMAL — WILD AND
UNPREDICTABLE.

METAL TIGER

For expressing opinions this roaring tiger is the
worst (or best) of them all. Very ambitious, it can be
a bit ruthless when it comes to its career. Don't
stand in the way of a metal tiger and never invest in
any of its schemes. This is a tiger for whom the
word "diplomacy" simply doesn't exist.

Tiger Compatibility Chart

TIGER WITH:

RAT
As neither of these two knows how to compromise, this combination will create sparks and the relationship will be stormy.

OX
Unless the tiger allows the ox to be in control and set the rules, this combination can't work. As tigers don't give in easily, expect fireworks.

TIGER
Expect a lot of heat – the heat of passion and ferocious lust. These two will fight and reconcile, laugh and love – a lot.

HARE
The hare makes a good meal for the tiger unless it learns to move fast to stay out of trouble. Although not a good combination, it can work.

DRAGON
Excitement and fun all the way. Dramatic and volatile. A super-charged dynamic team who together can move the earth.

SNAKE
The snake thinks the tiger is over-emotional, while the tiger distrusts the snake's secretive ways. This relationship is bound to end in disaster.

HORSE
A good combination. The tiger will respect the horse's loyalty and the horse will love the tiger's impulsiveness.

GOAT
Could be good together in bed, but there is not a lot else going for them. This partnership is not recommended for business.

MONKEY
As neither will give an inch, this is not a good combination. Both suffer ego problems and neither will understand the other at all.

ROOSTER
In spite of the fact that these two will bicker and quarrel, criticize and argue, this match is quite a good one.

DOG
The dog is clever enough to handle the tiger, so these two will do extremely well together.

PIG
These two blame each other when things go wrong and aren't really suited.

The Hare

Intuitive, psychic, sensitive, creative, hares care about others. They are lone souls who deeply feel the pain of the world and often try hard to put it all right. They love anything to do with mysteries and hidden knowledge, and are seekers after Truth. Invariably calm and moderate, quiet and refined, hares like to know secrets, which they are capable of keeping to themselves – annoyingly so. They make good counsellors and clairvoyants. They are well spoken and eloquent, and have good taste and a strong sense of style.

ELEMENT:

WOOD

YEARS OF THE HARE

1903 • 1915
1927 • 1939
1951 • 1963
1975 • 1987
1999 • 2011

CHARACTERISTICS

INTUITIVE
•
SENSITIVE
•
CARING
•
STYLISH
•
CALM

SUITABLE CAREERS

ACCOUNTANT
•
PHARMACIST
•
HISTORIAN
•
ART COLLECTOR
•
LIBRARIAN
•
DIPLOMAT

Hare Characteristics

Hares like to express their emotions and can be volatile if roused by cruelty or suffering. They have a strong sense of fair play but do like to break rules themselves, and they can be a bit arrogant, seeing themselves as a little superior to others. Hares possess genuine intuitive powers and need a calm stable atmosphere to thrive.

LOVE, SEX AND RELATIONSHIPS

Hares get hurt easily, often in love, so they can be very wary of becoming involved. Considerate, gentle lovers, with a true sense of kindness and romance, they will listen to a lover's problems and needs and do what they can to meet them. Hares are traditional and reserved in their sexual habits and are easily frightened by too much tension or intrigue. They prefer a romantic candlelit supper with their true love to an affair or a one-night stand. They are very moral and can be prudish.

BUSINESS, FRIENDS AND CHILDREN

Because of their sensitive nature and inherent good taste, hares will thrive in any business where they can use their flair for style and creativity. They suffer in routine jobs and need to work for themselves. They have many friends and will feel let down by all of them because no one can ever meet the high standards that hares set for themselves – and expect of others. As parents, hares are wonderfully calm and kind. They aren't very good with rowdy or badly behaved children, though, and can be very strict. They do inspire children to work hard, however, and children will adore them.

HARES ARE INTUITIVE ALMOST TO THE POINT OF CLAIRVOYANCE. THEY ARE ATTRACTED TO SECRETS AND MYSTERIES.

THE HARE IS TRADITIONAL, CULTURED, REFINED AND GENTLE.

THE HARE PARENT IS VERY LOVING, CALM AND KIND.

The Five Hare Types

WATER HARE
Doubly intuitive and doubly sensitive, the water hare can take on too much of others' troubles and get bogged down in suffering. It is prone to irrational fears and can become reclusive and withdrawn. It needs to be livened up occasionally.

WOOD HARE
Truly artistic with immense creativity, this hare is good with anything that lets it express emotion – poetry, literature, painting. It is the most adventurous of the hares, with a flair for travel and exotic locations.

FIRE HARE
This passionate hare has a very strong social conscience, works tirelessly for the good of the world and is a good political debater. It is very expressive and people will listen, and quite rightly so for it does know what's what.

EARTH HARE
This serious, studious, hard-working, quiet hare gets on with the job in hand and possesses a fine set of moral principles. It makes a good judge or social worker. This is a sensible, pragmatic, realistic and down-to-earth hare who sets its sights at an achievable level.

METAL HARE
Ambitious, with courage and perseverance, this least emotional of the hares will rise to lofty heights in any field where its vision and confidence can be put to good use.

THE FIRE HARE IS SOCIABLE AND ALSO MAKES A GOOD POLITICAL DEBATER.

THE WOOD HARE LIKES CULTURE, ART AND TRAVEL – AN ADVENTUROUS AND EXOTIC HARE.

THE EARTH HARE IS STUDIOUS AND HARD-WORKING.

Hare Compatibility Chart

HARE WITH:

RAT	The rat is a control freak while the hare dislikes control of any sort, so this is not a good combination at all.
OX	The hare has a natural optimism that won't suit the ox, who is pessimistic by nature. These two are badly suited.
TIGER	The hare makes a good meal for the tiger unless it learns to move fast to stay out of trouble. Although not a good combination, it can work.
HARE	These two understand each other perfectly which can make the union very good – or very bad. They will both walk away when things go badly.
DRAGON	The hare helps calm the dragon and they work well together as a team, especially as business partners.
SNAKE	With a lot in common, these two have a natural affinity. Not a lot of passion though.
HORSE	The horse is too impulsive and the hare too thoughtful – they will irritate each other. Not a good combination.
GOAT	As long as nothing goes wrong these two are harmonious and beautiful together. At the first sign of trouble they will not support each other, however.
MONKEY	These two characters are so completely alien to each other, a union can't work. They have nothing in common.
ROOSTER	The hare's stand-offishness will infuriate the rooster and the rooster's arrogance will alienate the hare. Not a good combination.
DOG	A nice combination. They understand and respect each other so the partnership works extremely well.
PIG	For some strange reason, these two always seem to get on well. Perhaps it is true that opposites attract – it is in this case.

The Dragon

YEARS OF THE
DRAGON

1904 • 1916
1928 • 1940
1952 • 1964
1976 • 1988
2000 • 2012

ELEMENT:

WOOD

Big, bright and bold, the dragon is life's good luck symbol. Dragons are glorious and mythical, confident and glamorous. They can also be vain and arrogant but you'll forgive them because they are so big and so wonderful that you cannot help but be impressed. They are also fickle and erratic, they love new things but quickly tire of them. This includes clothes, of which they must have many, and the brighter and more fashionable the better. Dragons are usually extremely energetic, full of life and fun. They like to be surrounded by friends and admirers, sycophants and lovers.

CHARACTERISTICS

SUCCESSFUL
•
INDEPENDENT
•
CONFIDENT
•
ENERGETIC
•
KIND

SUITABLE CAREERS

MANAGING DIRECTOR
•
TYCOON
•
FILM STAR
•
PRODUCER
•
PRESIDENT
•
FASHION DESIGNER

Dragon Characteristics

Dragons are bright, showy creatures with an endless enthusiasm for life, parties and kindness. Although they are generally very friendly and considerate of others, you must be careful never to anger one because you won't like the results – dragons really do breathe fire.

THE DRAGON LOVES DRESSING UP AND SHOWING OFF NEW PARTY CLOTHES.

LOVE, SEX AND RELATIONSHIPS

Dragons need more lovers than the world can provide. They get bored so quickly that anyone falling for a dragon had better know it will be short-lived. The only really true companion with any chance of a long-term relationship for a dragon is another dragon. If a dragon does ever fall in love – which may be a rare thing indeed – it will worship the loved one with a deep, possessive jealous love that is almost suffocating in its intensity. Dragons like sex, a lot, and will wear out any lover, except another dragon, with its demands.

DRAGONS NEED MANY LOVERS, AND WILL DEVOTE MUCH TIME TO PURSUING THEM

BUSINESS, FRIENDS AND CHILDREN

Dragons perform well in any field where they can be adored and admired – acting is good for them and they make marvellous celebrities. They also make good fashion designers, impresarios and producers. They are best heading a large corporation rather than working for someone else. Dragons will have many friends who have children, whom the dragons think are adorable. Dragons never think badly of children, but they try to avoid having any of their own – they simply can't stand all the mess and noise. Other people's children are fine for a short while as they can be handed back to their parents.

DRAGONS PERFORM WELL IN ANY FIELD WHERE THEY CAN BE ADORED AND ADMIRED.

The Five Dragon Types

WATER DRAGON

This idealistic dragon believes strongly in itself. These dragons can be very egotistical – they alone have the solution to the world's problems and can't understand why we aren't all listening to them, but they do genuinely care about others.

WOOD DRAGON

This beautiful dragon is an exquisite beast that is widely admired. A great trend-setter and leader of fashion, it is aloof and sophisticated, cool and stylish.

FIRE DRAGON

Bigger and brighter than any other dragon, this one is also very entertaining, amusing, friendly, witty, social and warm-hearted. It does possess a temper, though.

EARTH DRAGON

The only dragon who can work as part of a team, the earth dragon is more realistic and self-knowing than the other types. It is very conservative and traditional.

METAL DRAGON

The theatrical metal dragon is loud and showy, bright and glamorous. Although bombastic and opinionated, it is very entertaining and wonderfully colourful – truly eccentric.

THE FLAMBOYANT AND GLAMOROUS METAL DRAGON LOVES BEING SURROUNDED BY FRIENDS AND ADMIRERS.

THE WOOD DRAGON IS A TRENDSETTER – A DRAGON OF EXQUISITE TASTE.

THE FIRE DRAGON IS VERY SOCIABLE AND ENTERTAINING.

Dragon Compatibility Chart

DRAGON WITH:

RAT — A good relationship despite the apparent differences. Each will support the other in their schemes and will be able to give the other the attention they crave.

OX — A powerful combination. The ox can curb the dragon's impetuosity and if they work as a team they can achieve anything together.

TIGER — Excitement and fun all the way. Dramatic and volatile. A super-charged dynamic team who together can move the earth.

HARE — The hare helps calm the dragon and they work well together as a team, especially as business partners.

DRAGON — If they can learn to work together (unlikely) they get on very well. If not they fight (more likely).

SNAKE — A mystic union. They are both reptilian and understand the other well. A good combination.

HORSE — These two are a lot of fun together although they will fight and argue a lot. A very interesting pairing.

GOAT — Goats are attracted to dragons but get hurt in the process as dragons fail to see them – the indifference is hurtful.

MONKEY — A brilliant combination. These two are both clever, versatile and active. They both like to live by their wits and together they make a formidable partnership.

ROOSTER — A dramatic but good partnership. They both have big personalities but are sufficiently different to make the union interesting.

DOG — Bad news. These two positively dislike each other on sight. The relationship can't and won't work.

PIG — The dragon inspires the pig and the pair bounce off each other. The pig can get roasted, though, so it should keep a little in reserve.

YEARS OF THE
SNAKE

1905 • 1917
1929 • 1941
1953 • 1965
1977 • 1989
2001 • 2013

The Snake

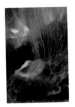

ELEMENT:

FIRE

Snakes are the philosophers and deep thinkers of the Chinese zodiac. They are mysterious, clever, shrewd and sensual. They can be cruel and remote but if given the right start in life (a sound education and good moral guidance) they are useful and extremely practical. Snakes can see solutions where others might not even see a problem. They are indulgent and sophisticated, and move with ease and grace – languid and very stylish. Snakes are wise people who have explored the deep mysteries of life and know a lot. They are clever without ever appearing to do any work.

CHARACTERISTICS

MYSTERIOUS
•
SOPHISTICATED
•
PRACTICAL
•
INDULGENT
•
WISE
•
ORGANIZED

SUITABLE CAREERS

PROFESSOR
•
ASTROLOGER
•
PSYCHOLOGIST
•
INTERIOR DESIGNER
•
PERSONNEL OFFICER
•
PHILOSOPHER

Snake Characteristics

Snakes are perpetually curious about the world and love anything esoteric and secret. They are incredibly well-organized and will find quick and efficient ways to get things done – and one of their best points is that they always finish the things they begin.

SNAKES ARE KNOWLEDGEABLE AND GREAT EXPLORERS OF HIDDEN MYSTERIES.

LOVE, SEX AND RELATIONSHIPS

Snakes are sensuous and enjoy their relationships. They delight in sex, particularly in all its darker aspects, and can be considered extreme by some. They can be cold lovers, though, because they have an innate aloofness and remoteness that could be considered arrogant. It's not arrogance, however, it's just that they are always busy thinking. Snakes are passionate and very intense. They feel things deeply and analyse everything. They can become too intense and overwhelming. They love to flirt and will often be unfaithful, but it's not because they don't love their partners – they just occasionally need to check that the old magic charm is still working.

SNAKES HAVE HYPNOTIC PERSONALITIES AND CAN BE ESPECIALLY FASCINATING TO THOSE THEY ARE TRYING TO WOO.

BUSINESS, FRIENDS AND CHILDREN

Snakes do well in any field of research, science and discovery. They make good scientists, philosophers and lecturers. They acquire lots of friends because they do like to hear confessions and have secrets revealed to them – they are brilliant listeners. Snakes can make vague parents as they find it hard to concentrate on the trivia of children's needs but they do inspire children to become educated and thoughtful and they will teach their children to love books. They are kind parents, if a little distant and remote.

SNAKES ARE EAGER TO PASS ON THEIR LOVE OF BOOKS AND LEARNING TO THEIR CHILDREN.

蛇

The Five Snake Types

WATER SNAKE
This honest snake possesses integrity and
a well-developed sense of fairness and honour.
The ability to see things from all points
of view makes this snake a wise counsellor
or a good arbitrator.

WOOD SNAKE
Imaginative and creative, the wood snake is
often a writer with a wonderful sense of
beauty and finesse. It may appear lazy
though and can be self-indulgent.

FIRE SNAKE
A dynamic snake with boundless energy,
this snake isn't quite so philosophically
minded as the others and can do well in
public life as it has a clearer
appreciation of reality.

EARTH SNAKE
A friendly, harmonious snake with a
great love of culture and social functions,
this is the party snake with charm,
wit and sophistication.
It is amazingly vague
and forgetful.

METAL SNAKE
This strong, perfectionist snake is
serious and hardworking with a
quick sharp brain. The metal snake
is invariably honest and
moral – even to the point of
being fanatical.

WOOD SNAKES ARE
IMAGINATIVE AND
CREATIVE AND MAKE
GOOD WRITERS.

THE EARTH SNAKE IS A
PARTY ANIMAL WITH A
GREAT LOVE OF CULTURE
AND SOCIAL FUNCTIONS.

THE WATER SNAKE IS
SOUGHT OUT
FOR GOOD ADVICE AND
ARBITRATION.

38

Snake Compatibility Chart

SNAKE WITH:

RAT
The snake's love of secrets and mysteries will inflame the rat to fits of jealousy and distrust. Not a good combination.

OX
A good long-lasting and stable relationship. The snake understands the ox and will encourage it to lighten up – the ox gives the snake stability.

TIGER
The snake thinks the tiger is over-emotional, while the tiger distrusts the snake's secretive ways. This relationship is bound to end in disaster.

HARE
With a lot in common, these two have a natural affinity. Not a lot of passion though.

DRAGON
A mystic union. They are both reptilian and understand the other well. A good combination.

SNAKE
They get along fine but shouldn't get romantically involved – they're both much too jealous.

HORSE
A good combination. They spark each other off and as long as they both know what the other is doing they get on fine.

GOAT
Only in exceptional circumstances can this combination work. It's much more likely to end in indifference as the two have different agendas.

MONKEY
These two mistrust each other, are jealous of each other, and have no real understanding of the other. Yes, the relationship is doomed to failure.

ROOSTER
Despite their differences these two get along just fine. There is friction but it is manageable.

DOG
The dog trusts the snake, which suits the snake just fine. An unlikely combination but one that works.

PIG
These two never make a good combination and will never be able to see the other's point of view.

The Horse

Friendly and communicative, horses are great givers, and incurable gossips and talkers. They are friendly, kind, generous, encouraging, supportive and well-liked, and appreciate sincerity, openness and honesty. Horses can talk just a little too much, however, and they're always so cheerful it can be irritating. They can also be somewhat irresponsible and careless. As long as they're having fun and are in the limelight, everything is fine, but if your attention shifts away from them they can become sulky and bored and that leads them into trouble.

ELEMENT:

FIRE

YEARS OF THE
HORSE

1906 • 1918
1930 • 1942
1954 • 1966
1978 • 1990
2002 • 2014

CHARACTERISTICS

HARDWORKING
•
FRIENDLY
•
GENEROUS
•
TALKATIVE
•
CHEERFUL
•
BOISTEROUS

SUITABLE CAREERS

REPORTER
•
INVENTOR
•
TECHNICIAN
•
COMEDIAN
•
WINE EXPERT
•
RACING DRIVER

Horse Characteristics

Horses shy away from anything subversive or dark and prefer plain speaking to any coded messages – they're not very good at picking up hints. This doesn't mean that they're thick-skinned, just unaware of subtleties and have little notion of tact or discretion. They can be a bit boisterous and overpowering but they have hearts of gold and are genuinely nice people.

HORSES IN LOVE QUICKLY BECOME BORED UNLESS THERE IS CONSTANT ATTENTION FROM THEIR PARTNERS.

LOVE, SEX AND RELATIONSHIPS

A happy horse is one that is in love – and horses are usually happy. They do love to be in love. They are big softies, very romantic and charming. They can be impatient as lovers, however, and have a tendency to rush things. Although enthusiastic and exciting lovers, they can become bored easily if the magic and romance begins to wane. They enjoy all the physical aspects of love-making and are energetic lovers.

BUSINESS, FRIENDS ıD CHILDREN

Horses and money never go well together. Horses are frivolous and, as they never think of tomorrow, they do not accumulate any savings. Being creative and talented, anything to do with business does not appeal to them. They are social and popular – especially among other horses, and have many friends – good ones. They can be very good with children as long as they are outdoors and where nothing can get broken. Horses are notoriously clumsy and their boisterousness can sometimes frighten timid children.

HORSES ARE VERY ROMANTIC AND LOVE TO INDULGE THEIR PARTNERS.

HORSES HAVE AN ENDEARINGLY FRIVOLOUS SIDE TO THEIR PERSONALITIES.

The Five Horse Types

WATER HORSE
This truly artistic horse is very communicative
and witty, with a tremendous sense of fun.
Although very charming, it can be
a bit insensitive.

WOOD HORSE
Calmer and more reserved than the water
horse, the wood horse is slightly gullible and
can get teased a lot. But it is always jolly
and rarely gets depressed.

FIRE HORSE
In Chinese horoscopes this extreme
horse is either feared or famed. It either
rises to incredible heights or sinks to the lowest
depths. The fire horse year occurs only every
60 years and the next isn't until 2026.

THE METAL HORSE IS A
PASSIONATE CHARACTER, WHO
CRAVES ADMIRATION AND
ATTENTION.

EARTH HORSE
This is a stable and conventional horse with
traditional views and a rigid set of morals.
Earth horses can be a bit pompous but do
pay attention to detail and are relatively
well-organized.

METAL HORSE
Headstrong and easily bored, this horse
needs a lot of excitement and passion.
It is the Don Juan of horses and needs
many admirers and lovers.

THE WATER HORSE CAN
BE SWEET AND CHARMING,
BUT ALSO INSENSITIVE
AT TIMES.

Horse Compatibility Chart

HORSE WITH:

RAT — Neither partner will get a word in edgeways – but if either can learn to listen the relationship does have potential.

OX — The ox is thorough and methodical, while the horse is impulsive and rash. These two will irritate each other continually. Not a good combination.

TIGER — A good combination. The tiger will respect the horse's loyalty and the horse will love the tiger's impulsiveness.

HARE — Not a good combination. As the horse is too impulsive and the hare too thoughtful they will irritate each other.

DRAGON — These two are a lot of fun together although they will fight and argue a lot. A very interesting pairing.

SNAKE — These two spark each other off and as long as they both know what the other is doing they get on fine. A good combination.

HORSE — Not a very emotional pairing but one that can work extremely well. They both love their freedom and trust one another.

GOAT — These two can learn a lot from one another, and they have the potential to give a lot as well. A good combination.

MONKEY — After the initial cut and thrust for dominance has taken place, this is a very long-term, lasting relationship.

ROOSTER — The horse hates arguing and the rooster loves arguing, so these two can never really get on.

DOG — A brilliant relationship under any circumstances. These two understand each other almost telepathically.

PIG — The horse's popularity will enhance the pig's social standing – which the pig will appreciate. A good combination.

1907 • 1919
1931 • 1943
1955 • 1967
1979 • 1991
2003 • 2015

CHARACTERISTICS

ADAPTABLE
•
SEXY
•
CREATIVE
•
FRIENDLY
•
INDEPENDENT
•
CURIOUS

The Goat

Of all the animal signs the goat is the one best able to live in the moment. Goats don't fret about the past and they don't worry about the future. They are relaxed, happy-go-lucky creatures who like to enjoy what they have now rather than strive for what might be. They like to relax and be peaceful. Goats are creative and friendly and certainly like to meet people and talk a lot. They are kind, sincere, honest and imaginative. Nothing is too much trouble if it helps other people. Goats have a certain elegance and style about them.

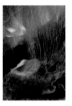

ELEMENT:
FIRE

SUITABLE CAREERS

TELEVISION PRESENTER
•
SEX COUNSELLOR
•
MUSICIAN
•
ARTIST
•
GARDEN DESIGNER
•
ACTOR

Goat Characteristics

Goats can be fiercely independent creatures and they hate being hemmed in or having their freedom curtailed. They need new people, fresh horizons and new experiences and excitements. They like to partake of all that life has to offer – they are perpetually curious and this can lead them into trouble.

LOVE, SEX AND RELATIONSHIPS

Goats have a capacity for making lovers feel very special – as if they are the only and true one. However, the goat will have many lovers and will try very hard never to settle down or be in a permanent relationship, which looks like a trap to them. They are adventurous when it comes to sex and like a lot of variety and experimentation. Goats aren't particularly moral and shouldn't be judged by conventional standards.

GOATS HAVE A TALENT FOR MAKING THEIR LOVERS FEEL SPECIAL, DESPITE THEIR AVERSION TO SETTLING DOWN.

BUSINESS, FRIENDS AND CHILDREN

Because of their charm and elegance, people are sometimes jealous of goats, but those who know goats well realize they have a good heart and care a lot about their friends. Goats in business are rare – in fact goats who work hard for long hours are rare. They are not lazy; just not motivated by money. They can be extremely busy and industrious when they want to be but the project has to either be creative or to benefit humankind in some way. Children adore goats as they will take time and trouble to talk to children without patronising them, and will go out of their way to treat them with the same respect as an adult.

GOATS HAVE A SPECIAL ATTRACTION FOR CHILDREN.

45

The Five Goat Types

WATER GOAT

This conservative goat dislikes change or other kind of upheaval. It is very sympathetic and takes the world's worries on its shoulders. It is sensitive and emotionally perceptive.

WOOD GOAT

A very sensitive, generous goat with great compassion, its inspirational talents would make it an excellent leader of a new religion.

FIRE GOAT

Courageous and intuitive with a good sense of drama, this goat would make a fine actor. It can be reckless and foolhardy, however, and should never be trusted with large amounts of money – its own or anyone else's.

EARTH GOAT

This goat likes fine, rare and beautiful objects and enjoys good art. It would make an excellent art critic or collector of antiques.

METAL GOAT

Determined and ambitious, the metal goat enjoys a particularly thick skin and is impervious to criticism. This goat will go at anything relentlessly.

THE WOOD GOAT IS A COMPASSIONATE CHARACTER WITH A DEEP SENSITIVITY TOWARDS OTHERS.

THE FIRE GOAT'S SENSE OF DRAMA MAKES IT A NATURAL ACTOR.

THE EARTH GOAT LOVES FINE ART AND ANTIQUES AND WILL COLLECT AVIDLY IF ITS CIRCUMSTANCES ALLOW.

Goat Compatibility Chart

GOAT WITH:

RAT — If the rat is allowed to control and be in charge then this could be a successful union. However, if the goat wants any freedom, the relationship is doomed.

OX — These two won't agree on anything, and the ox will be appalled by the goat's apparent lack of morals.

TIGER — Could be good together in bed, but there is not a lot else going for them. This partnership is not recommended for business.

HARE — As long as nothing goes wrong these two are harmonious and beautiful together. At the first sign of trouble they will not support each other, however.

DRAGON — Goats are attracted to dragons but get hurt in the process as dragons fail to see them – the indifference is hurtful.

SNAKE — Only in exceptional circumstances can this combination work. It's much more likely to end in indifference as the two have different agendas.

HORSE — These two can learn a lot from one another, and they have the potential to give a lot as well. A good combination.

GOAT — One of this pair will need to take control – and that's the problem. Neither is any good at being in charge and together they will go nowhere.

MONKEY — This isn't a bad partnership. The monkey motivates the goat and the goat curbs the monkey's excesses.

ROOSTER — The rooster will never allow the goat time off, while the goat will be irritated by the rooster's flamboyance.

DOG — These two can tolerate each other well but there's little passion between them and little understanding.

PIG — Each of these leads the other astray, which can be fine but is not really conducive to a lasting relationship.

The Monkey

YEARS OF THE
MONKEY

1908 • 1920
1932 • 1944
1956 • 1968
1980 • 1992
2004 • 2016

Inquisitive, bright, energetic and highly competitive, the monkey is the liveliest of the animal signs – full of new ideas, and always scheming, mainly to get its own way. Monkeys are very good at manipulating other people. They make fine leaders – as long as people realize that where they are being led is entirely at the whim of the monkey – and they always have their own agenda. Monkeys have quick, sharp brains and are usually extremely sharp-witted and clever – this isn't to say they are necessarily wise, but they are always clever.

ELEMENT:
METAL

CHARACTERISTICS

QUICK-WITTED
•
ENTERTAINING
•
INQUISITIVE
•
ENERGETIC
•
MANIPULATIVE
•
OPTIMISTIC

SUITABLE CAREERS

JOURNALIST
•
TEACHER
•
ENTREPRENEUR
•
TRAVEL WRITER
•
THERAPIST

Monkey Characteristics

Monkeys are social creatures who love having lots of people around them. They are also, however, independent characters, and are always optimistic. They like to take risks and will always rise to a challenge – or a dare. The monkey is loud and communicative, full of itself and very entertaining.

MONKEYS LOVE LARGE GATHERINGS OF PEOPLE AND BIG SOCIAL OCCASIONS.

LOVE, SEX AND RELATIONSHIPS
Monkeys have voracious appetites both for relationships and for sex. They enjoy the challenge of new conquests and love the experience of being in love. They seem to achieve their best potential while in a relationship, but their interest, as in all things, will quickly turn to something – or someone – else if their interest isn't kept up – they need fresh excitement continually. Monkeys have no moral code and will stray at any opportunity. They hate conflict in any relationship and will run at the first sign of trouble.

BUSINESS, FRIENDS AND CHILDREN
Monkeys collect large numbers of friends, and small children will follow them to the ends of the earth. Business partners will drop them quite quickly, however, when they attempt to follow any of the monkey's crazier schemes – of which there will be many. Monkeys and money are easily separated. Monkeys change careers often and quickly, as they hate routine. They can shine in any occupation where they can use their wits, be inventive and entertaining and don't have to work too hard. The monkey is, by nature, quite indolent.

MONKEYS ENJOY INDULGING THEIR APPETITE FOR SEXUAL RELATIONSHIPS.

MONKEYS' SEXUAL APPETITES WILL LEAD THEM TO STRAY OFTEN AND WITHOUT COMPUNCTION.

The Five Monkey Types

WATER MONKEY
You won't ever understand this secret monkey, full of hidden agendas and complex mysteries. It is a monkey from another planet. It is affectionate but keeps its distance. It can be a worrier and take slights to heart.

WOOD MONKEY
A truly resourceful monkey, very talented, artistic and creative, this is the cleverest of all the monkeys. It is the friendliest monkey too, and is very warm and lovable.

FIRE MONKEY
This passionate lover monkey is very dynamic, charming and ruthless, and needs more lovers than there are available. Very dangerous, but very attractive.

EARTH MONKEY
More harmonious than the other monkeys, this is the great communicator. It is extremely witty and very funny although its humour can verge on the cruel. Its parodies are extremely accurate, if unkind.

METAL MONKEY
This monkey loves to take risks. It may well be a gambler and may be the only monkey that can make money. It is very independent, hates to be tied down and will escape any traps laid for it.

THE WOOD MONKEY'S ARTISTIC TALENTS MAY LEAD TO A LOVE OF MUSICAL PERFORMANCE.

THE PENSIVE WATER MONKEY KEEPS ITS DISTANCE FROM OTHERS AND IS FULL OF SECRECY.

THE METAL MONKEY IS A RISK TAKER WHO MAY ENJOY THE THRILL OF GAMBLING.

Monkey Compatibility Chart

MONKEY WITH:

RAT
These two characters are similar in personality and will do well together. They are both starters rather than finishers and so will need to make allowances for that to do well together.

OX
The monkey constantly seeks change and the ox hates it. This combination can't work under any circumstances.

TIGER
As neither will give an inch, this is not a good combination. Both suffer ego problems and neither will understand the other at all.

HARE
These two are so completely alien to each other, a union can't work. They have nothing in common.

DRAGON
These two are both clever, versatile and active. They both like to live by their wits and together they make a formidable partnership. A brilliant combination.

SNAKE
These two mistrust each other, are jealous of each other, and have no real understanding of the other. Yes, the relationship is doomed to failure.

HORSE
After the initial cut and thrust for dominance has taken place, this is a very long-term, lasting relationship.

GOAT
These two can learn a lot from each other, and they have the potential to give a lot as well. A good combination.

MONKEY
Too much rivalry. Too much competition. This combination could settle into a team but it is unlikely.

ROOSTER
If they share any interest they can get along – but that is not really a basis for a love match.

DOG
If these two have any common interests they get on well but basically they do not make a good combination.

PIG
A good team for indulgence. They both like pleasure and excitement and get on well together. Not a good combination though if there are any serious problems.

The Rooster

Roosters like to show off. They are flamboyant, colourful people with outgoing personalities and a friendly way about them. They are good communicators and enthusiastic. They do like to be independent although they are fond of their families. They can be very entertaining as they are never still or quiet, but most of their stories will be about them and their prowess in whatever activity they excel at. Roosters are far more sensitive than you'd ever know – or they will ever show – and they can be deeply hurt by criticism.

YEARS OF THE
ROOSTER

1909 • 1921
1933 • 1945
1957 • 1969
1981 • 1993
2005 • 2017

ELEMENT:
METAL

CHARACTERISTICS

PROTECTIVE
•
HONEST
•
FLAMBOYANT
•
ENTERTAINING
•
SENSITIVE

SUITABLE CAREERS

ENGINEER
•
BEAUTICIAN
•
SURGEON
•
COMPANY DIRECTOR
•
HAIRDRESSER
•
PUBLIC RELATIONS

Rooster Characteristics

Roosters put great store by education, and will read and learn a lot by themselves. They often know more than you think, although they don't like to appear too clever. They often play the part of the buffoon when they don't need to – it's just another way of getting attention. Roosters can be quite insecure deep down.

ROOSTERS LIKE TO BE SURROUNDED BY PEOPLE BUT THEIR GREGARIOUSNESS CAN HIDE INSECURITY.

ROOSTERS RECOGNIZE THE VALUE OF A GOOD EDUCATION AND WILL LEARN AS MUCH AS THEY CAN.

LOVE, SEX AND RELATIONSHIPS

Love is a serious business for roosters and when they take a partner they expect it to last – for life. They are not, however, necessarily completely faithful themselves but they do expect their partners to be. They are dramatic and exciting lovers and have endless sexual energy but little imagination. Roosters expect a lot from their partners, and can be quite hard to be with in a relationship, especially as they don't like to give too much away about themselves in return.

BUSINESS, FRIENDS AND CHILDREN

Roosters like to be surrounded by people but probably wouldn't call any of them friends. Although roosters will certainly have many acquaintances, they don't really ever open up sufficiently for friendships to develop. Roosters adore children and can give them considerable attention while still working hard themselves – a unique skill. Roosters have an infinite capacity for hard work which makes them very popular with employers. They love a challenge and will often enter an occupation for which they seem unsuited, and will then slog heroically away at it until it is conquered.

ROOSTERS ARE EAGER TO LEARN NEW SKILLS AND WILL WORK HARD AT WHATEVER THEY DO.

A FORMAL CHINESE WEDDING WOULD BE VERY SUITABLE FOR THE ROOSTER – THEY TAKE LOVE AND MARRIAGE VERY SERIOUSLY.

The Five Rooster Types

WATER ROOSTER
One of the few roosters that can work in
a team, this is a sympathetic, caring
rooster who takes on world causes.
A kinder, calmer rooster.

WOOD ROOSTER
With masses of enthusiasm, the very
extroverted wood rooster can be highly
creative but is also prone to live life excessively
and may overdo anything it takes on.

THE THEATRICAL WOOD
ROOSTER IS HIGHLY
CREATIVE WITH A
TENDENCY TO EXCESS.

FIRE ROOSTER
This dramatic, flamboyant rooster can
be very successful if it can curb its aggressive
streak. It has a unique ability to be able to see
into the future and plan accordingly, which
can make it a bit reckless as it thinks
it is all-knowing.

EARTH ROOSTER
The earth rooster is a very determined,
blunt rooster of few words. It can be disliked
for its forthright opinions but it is usually right.
It takes its responsibilities seriously and
can be very ambitious.

THE RECKLESS FIRE
ROOSTER HAS A TENDENCY
TO AGGRESSION WHICH IT
NEEDS TO CONTROL.

METAL ROOSTER
As it sets very high standards indeed, this
rooster won't tolerate fools and expects
everyone to live up to its ideals. It is rather
inflexible and can suffer as a result. This
rooster needs to learn to relax
and will find times when it needs
to be on its own.

THE METAL ROOSTER'S HIGH
EXPECTATIONS OF OTHERS
WILL RESULT IN THE NEED FOR
QUIET CONTEMPLATION,
ALONE, AT TIMES.

Rooster Compatibility Chart

ROOSTER WITH:

RAT

With two control freaks, this combination just can't work. Neither partner will be interested in the other and both will demand to be in charge.

OX

The rooster sets things in motion and the ox will see them through. A good combination.

TIGER

In spite of the fact that these two will bicker and quarrel, criticise and argue, this match is quite a good one.

HARE

The hare's stand-offishness will infuriate the rooster and the rooster's arrogance will alienate the hare. Not a good combination.

DRAGON

A dramatic but good partnership. They both have big personalities but are sufficiently different to make the union interesting.

SNAKE

Despite their differences these two get along just fine. There is friction but it is manageable.

HORSE

The horse hates arguing and the rooster loves arguing, so these two can never really get on.

GOAT

The rooster will never allow the goat time off, while the goat will be irritated by the rooster's flamboyance.

MONKEY

If they share any interests they can get along but that is not really a basis for a love match.

ROOSTER

This couple will bicker and criticize each other but they can get on well – they can also fight. Overall, not really a good match.

DOG

The dog will eventually get bored waiting for the rooster to calm down, and the rooster will be irritated by the dog's patience. Not a good combination.

PIG

Although different, these two can be friends. They share similar interests and can have an interesting, if passionless, relationship.

The Dog

Years of the Dog

1910 • 1922
1934 • 1946
1958 • 1970
1982 • 1994
2006 • 2018

Of the all the Chinese animals the dog is the friendliest and kindest. Dogs are here to serve us all and they love being of use. They understand loyalty and faithfulness in ways others could only dream of. It is no accident that the dog was chosen to represent this group of people for the dog is a firm, dutiful, noble beast indeed – and so are these people. Dog people are unselfish and moral. They love to be with other people and are extremely honest, trustworthy and tolerant. They are easy to take advantage of, and they can overdo their good aspects.

Element:

Metal

Characteristics

Loyal
•
Trustworthy
•
Friendly
•
Kind
•
Unselfish
•
Fatalistic

Suitable Careers

Critic
•
Lawyer
•
Doctor
•
Priest
•
Professor
•
Charity worker

Dog Characteristics

Dogs are eager to please, perhaps too eager, too ready to help, too anxious to serve. They can also be a bit unadventurous and can suffer from a kind of victim mentality where everything that goes wrong is endured with fatalism and stoicism. If left to their own devices they can run wild – they need to be supervised and led.

DOGS SEEK COMPANIONSHIP AND ARE QUITE CONTENT WITH PLATONIC, RATHER THAN SEXUAL, RELATIONSHIPS.

LOVE, SEX AND RELATIONSHIPS

Although dogs are into romance and love in a big way they enjoy friendly relationships much more. They seek companionship rather than sex and would be quite happy to keep all their affairs platonic. Their need to please, however, makes them good lovers as they go out of their way to be approved of and praised. They are quite faithful but do need a lot of reassurance that they are still loved. They can be very jealous and suspicious lovers which can lead them to destroy a relationship unintentionally.

DOGS NEED PLENTY OF REASSURANCE FROM THEIR PARTNERS AND WORRY ABOUT WHETHER THEY ARE STILL LOVED.

BUSINESS, FRIENDS AND CHILDREN

Of all the zodiac signs children would rather be with a dog than any other. Dogs are big kids at heart themselves. They have few really close friends but everyone loves a dog in their own way. Dogs are very outgoing social people who need constant contact and company. This is probably best seen in their love of children, whom they adore. Dogs are extremely hard workers and can rise to any challenge. They work well in teams and will shoulder responsibility well. They don't particularly like to lead and need to be encouraged by their colleagues, and given specific tasks to perform.

DOGS ARE GOOD TEAM WORKERS AND HAVE A STRONG SENSE OF DUTY TO THEIR COMMUNITY.

The Five Dog Types

WATER DOG

The happiest dog of all likes being outdoors and makes a good farmer or gardener. This is a more relaxed dog, charming and sociable, and one who can be slightly more liberal than the other types.

WOOD DOG

The creative wood dog is extremely talented and can make a most wonderful home environment. It is very intuitive and can empathize with the needs and problems of others.

THE WATER DOG IS A RELAXED, SOCIAL DOG WHO LIKES TO BE OUTDOORS; THESE DOGS MAKE GOOD GARDENERS AND FARMERS.

FIRE DOG

This mad, flamboyant and colourful dog is loved and idealized for its kindness and warmth. It is brilliant with children, has infinite patience and resources and still has time for an unusual career.

EARTH DOG

Well-balanced and with materialistic ambitions, the earth dog is capable of considerable success, especially in the world of entertainment, as it possesses natural charisma.

THE WOOD DOG WILL PUT A LOT OF EFFORT INTO CREATING A HAPPY AND SECURE HOME ENVIRONMENT.

METAL DOG

This guard dog can bite. Although it can be very principled, strong and determined, it is still essentially a dog and likes to be liked.

THE EARTH DOG IS A NATURAL ENTERTAINER WITH GREAT CHARISMA.

Dog Compatibility Chart

DOG WITH:

RAT — A good team. The rat's control and the dog's loyalty make a good combination. They both like to talk a lot though.

OX — If both partners share the same goals, this can be a good partnership, but in business rather than love.

TIGER — The dog is clever enough to handle the tiger, so these two will do extremely well together.

HARE — A nice combination. They understand and respect each other so the partnership works extremely well.

DRAGON — These two positively dislike each other on sight. The relationship can't and won't work.

SNAKE — The dog trusts the snake, which suits the snake just fine. An unlikely combination but one that works.

HORSE — A brilliant relationship under any circumstances. These two understand each other almost telepathically.

GOAT — They can tolerate each other well but there's little passion between them and little understanding.

MONKEY — If these two have any common interests they get on well but basically they do not make a good combination.

ROOSTER — The dog will eventually get bored waiting for the rooster to calm down, and the rooster will be irritated by the dog's patience. Not a good combination.

DOG — They may love each other forever – or fight on sight. The union is risky but worth it if it works.

PIG — No real conflicts, although the pig's spending habits may baffle the thrifty, honest dog.

The Pig

Pigs love pleasure but what their pleasures are may be hard for other signs to understand. We might not like to roll around in mud but they do. And for mud read emotional turmoil. Pigs need to know all about themselves emotionally, so they can tend to be a bit self-indulgent. But they do have big hearts and care a lot about other people. They are very forgiving and always seek a quiet and peaceful life even to the point of being withdrawn from the mainstream, preferring instead to stay at home and indulge themselves.

YEARS OF THE PIG

1911 • 1923
1935 • 1947
1959 • 1971
1983 • 1995
2007 • 2019

ELEMENT:
WATER

CHARACTERISTICS

SENSUAL
•
EAGER
•
PLEASURE-SEEKING
•
MORAL
•
VIRTUOUS

SUITABLE CAREERS

CHEF
•
HEALER
•
COUNSELLOR
•
DIPLOMAT
•
CIVIL SERVANT
•
ARCHITECT

Pig Characteristics

Pigs are moral beasts; clean in their habits and avoiding anything dark or dangerous. They expect others to follow their strict virtuous guidelines and are surprised when they don't. Pigs have good common sense and their advice will often be sought and followed. Pigs are natural mediators and diplomats.

LOVE, SEX AND RELATIONSHIPS

Pigs will do anything to keep their partners happy – until they have had enough and then they become boars. A roused pig is dangerous and should be avoided. Pigs are happy in love and need a good partner who will allow them the space and freedom to explore their own emotional needs – they will, however rarely find this. Because of their own inward turning they will often miss the warning signs of a relationship dwindling due to lack of attention.

BUSINESS, FRIENDS AND CHILDREN

Pigs have many friends as they are popular and keep a good table. They love to cook for friends and their advice will often be asked for. Children find pigs a bit hard to take as they can be very strict and set such high standards. A pig in business is a rare sight indeed. Pigs think it better to let others do all the hard work and keep them well supplied with everything they need. Pigs do expect a lot from others including being looked after. Pigs need security and will plan for it. They don't take risks and they like comfort and harmony in their lives.

PIGS ARE GOOD COOKS AND LOVE ENTERTAINING AND FEEDING THEIR MANY FRIENDS.

PIGS' DIPLOMATIC SKILLS MEAN THEY ARE OFTEN SOUGHT OUT FOR ADVICE AND MEDIATION.

PIGS ENJOY STAYING AT HOME AND TAKING ADVANTAGE OF ITS PEACE AND SECURITY.

The Five Pig Types

WATER PIG
This self-indulgent pig needs to
be got out of bed and made to work
hard or it will wallow forever. In spite
of its lazy, good-for-nothing habits,
however, this is a charmer.

WOOD PIG
Wise and ambitious, this powerful
pig can achieve great success,
if it is not taken advantage
of along the way.

FIRE PIG
Brave and adventurous, this
pig likes to take risks –
little ones but with
dramatic consequences.

EARTH PIG
Whatever happens outside, in the
big wide world, this prudent,
home-loving pig will invariably be safe
and secure inside.

METAL PIG
Witty and entertaining,
this party pig doesn't like to
stay at home for too long. As long as there
are good food and fine wines you'll not
be rid of the metal pig. It is very
sociable and friendly – until your
cupboard is bare and then it will
quietly slip away, only to return another
day when your stocks are replenished.

THE LIKEABLE WATER PIG
NEEDS ENCOURAGEMENT TO
STIR ITSELF, AND WILL
HAPPILY LIE AROUND ALL
DAY IF ALLOWED.

THE WOOD PIG MAKES A
GOOD AMBASSADOR AND HAS
THE POTENTIAL TO BECOME
VERY POWERFUL.

THE METAL PIG ENJOYS
PARTIES AND WILL BE THE
LAST TO LEAVE A SOCAL
GATHERING.

Pig Compatibility Chart

PIG WITH:

RAT If the rat can earn it, the pig can spend it. As long as both know where they stand this is a good partnership.

OX The ox will never tolerate the pig's spending habits, and the pig will consider the ox dull. Not a promising union.

TIGER These two blame each other when things go wrong and aren't really suited.

HARE For some strange reason these two always seem to get on well. Perhaps it is true that opposites attract – it is in this case.

DRAGON The dragon inspires the pig and the pair bounce off each other. The pig can get roasted, though, so it should keep a little in reserve.

SNAKE These two make a good combination if they ever manage to see the other's point of view.

HORSE The horse's popularity will enhance the pig's social standing – which the pig will appreciate. A good combination.

GOAT Each of these leads the other astray, which can be fine but is not really conducive to a lasting relationship.

MONKEY A good team for indulgence. They both like pleasure and excitement and get on well together. Not a good combination though if there are any serious problems.

ROOSTER Although different these two can be friends. They share similar interests and can have an interesting, if passionless, relationship.

DOG No real conflicts, although the pig's spending habits may baffle the poor thrifty dog.

PIG These two can be friends but nothing more. They both rather like to over-indulge which isn't the basis for a lasting love affair.

THIS BOOK IS DEDICATED TO OLIVER BUSH

Acknowledgements

The publishers would like to thank the following libraries for the use of their pictures:

ET Archive
6L: Guimet Museum, Paris; 6M: Guimet Museum, Paris; 8R: British Museum; 18TR: National Library, Australia; 21TL: Civic Museum of Ascoli Piceno; 33BR; 38TR; 61L: Conde Chantilly Museum; 61TR: Trier State Museum.

Visual Arts Library
7L; 11TR: Edimedia/Phillips Fine Art Auctioneer; 18ML; 20L; 21BL; 22MR; 25TL: Estampe Collection; 26BL: Guimet Museum; 29BL; 34R; 38BR; 45TR; 46BL; 50L: Victoria and Albert Museum, London; 50BR; 53BL; 58BR; 61BR; 62BL: Back Jacket Flap.

Bruce Coleman
9TL: Kim Taylor; 9TR: Peter Terry; 9BR: Stephen J Doyle; 9M.

Fine Art Photographic
17TL; 17BR; 17R: Colin Stodgell; 21R: Anthony Mitchell Paintings, Nottingham; 22TL: Anthony Mitchell Paintings, Nottingham; 25BL: Haynes Fine Art; 25MR: Haynes Fine Art; 26R: John Noott Galleries; 29L; 29TR: Anthony Mitchell Paintings, Nottingham; 29BR; 30TL; 29R; 33ML: Berko Gallery; 33TR: Sutcliffe Galleries, Harrogate; 34TL; 34BL; 37L: Berko Gallery; 37TR; 37BR; 38L; 41L: Anthony Mitchell Paintings, Nottingham; 41TR; 42BL: Bubenik; 42TR: Gavin Graham Gallery; 45L: Berko Gallery; 45BR: Anthony Mitchell Paintings, Nottingham; 46R: Berko Gallery; 49L: Colin Stodgell Gallery; 49TR: Cambridge Fine Art; 49BR; 50TR; 53TL: Ebury Galleries; 53TR; 54TL; 54BL: Adam Levene; 57TL: Fine Art of Oakham; 57BL: Martyn Gregory; 57R; 58L: Waterhouse and Dodd; 58TR: Anthony Mitchell Fine Paintings; 62TL: Berko Gallery; 62R.

L=Left, R=Right, T=Top, B=Bottom, M=Middle.